Curses and Verses

Curses and Verses

Andrew Casey

Copyright © 2014 Andrew Casey

The moral right of the author has been asserted.

Apart from any fair dealing for the purposes of research or private study, or criticism or review, as permitted under the Copyright, Designs and Patents Act 1988, this publication may only be reproduced, stored or transmitted, in any form or by any means, with the prior permission in writing of the publishers, or in the case of reprographic reproduction in accordance with the terms of licences issued by the Copyright Licensing Agency. Enquiries concerning reproduction outside those terms should be sent to the publishers.

Matador
9 Priory Business Park,
Wistow Road, Kibworth Beauchamp,
Leicestershire. LE8 0RX
Tel: (+44) 116 279 2299
Fax: (+44) 116 279 2277
Email: books@troubador.co.uk
Web: www.troubador.co.uk/matador

ISBN 978 1784620 295

British Library Cataloguing in Publication Data.
A catalogue record for this book is available from the British Library.

Typeset in 11pt Aldine401 BT Roman by Troubador Publishing Ltd, Leicester, UK
Printed and bound in the UK by TJ International, Padstow, Cornwall

Matador is an imprint of Troubador Publishing Ltd

This book is dedicated to my dear mother, Joyce, whose love of the arts in general and of poetry, in particular, inspired me to write. Also to Marina and Victoria, my lovely girls, and Olly my dog, who have all endured me for so many years.

Contents

Preface		ix
1.	Time	1
2.	She	2
3.	The Battlefield	3
4.	Olly	4
5.	New Age?	5
6.	First Doubts	6
7.	Lady	7
8.	Gone	8
9.	Dawn Rendezvous	9
10.	All Done	10
11.	A Public House in England	11
12.	London Life	12
13.	Caribbean Queen	13
14.	Visions of Old Age	14
15.	You	15
16.	Highams Lake	16
17.	The Ghosts	17
18.	Checkmate	19
19.	My Neighbour's Cat	20
20.	Foolish	21
21.	Heaven to Me	22

22. Images	23
23. Missing You	24
24. A Daughter's Plea	25
25. Noble King	26
26. One Day Soon	27
27. Bird on the Wing	28
28. Angel	29
29. End Game	30
30. Reflections of War	31
31. My Love	32
32. Wild Country	33
33. A Dog's Life	34
34. Air Hostess	35
35. Dark Times	36
36. Death by Taxi	37
37. Empty	38
38. Faking It	39
39. Forward	40
40. Night Raid	41
41. Our Love	42
42. The Body in Question	43
43. Thinking of You	44
44. Waiting	45
45. Where's the Girl?	46
46. Who Are You?	47
47. Life	49
48. We Shall Meet Again	50
Notes	51
A request from the author	65

Preface

These poems are a selection of those I have composed during my life, from "Battlefield" and "Reflections of War" both written when I was 14, to "The Ghosts" written some 40 years later. All have a meaning for me and I hope that one, at least, may strike a chord with someone out there.

Andrew Casey
Highams Park 2014.

Time

Shake off your drowsy sleep, face the new dawn as if it is your last,
put aside all thoughts of make-believe, enter the real world with all
　　its twisted paths.
Don't raise your hopes too high, lest the end result is far from what
　　you desire,
just make each day as painless as the last, for no greater happiness is
　　it possible to aspire.

Catch some time, never trade it for all the eloquence in England.
Hold it close, don't consider the possible consequence of its end.
Look back on each deeply held memory and preserve them completely.
For a pauper can become a king easier than a dying man can find a friend.

If you feel the whole uneven struggle is more than worthless,
whisper it softly, for that knowledge is not so obvious to the rest.
Treat each passing stranger with more than a passing politeness,
as the Devil in many guises may provide the final test.

She

Glittering tears cascade through tangled hair,
innocent eyes torment as fingers grasp at a drowning man's straw,
clutching to the bitter end that naïve disastrous faith,
regretting a hundred lonely moments, a millennium of heartache,
    the agony of life.

Still she dreams of what could be,
refusing to accept the reality of what is,
brushing aside stark unpalatable facts,
which she sees as the only hindrance to her goal.

Stretching her imagination to breaking point,
the future success and ultimate triumph assured.
Eyes blinkered, ears deaf, mind manacled,
friends unnoticed in the inevitability of the end,
until that final shattering blow of complete disaster
defeats her utterly as she always knew it would.

The Battlefield

The armies were lining the field for the battle, both horses and men herded like cattle
down to the battlefield, down to the mire, passed the stark bodies and into the fire.
The enemy were pressing, the hill for to gain, men wracked with fever, misery and pain,
fought like devils to hold that hill, bullets and bayonets could not move them still.
But it was madness, a hopeless position, the commanding officer made the vital decision.
Men, you are the bravest I have ever led, but we will have to retreat, retreat, he said,
but too late, the foe were advancing, men on foot and horses prancing.
One last thing did the officer say, Men, we will die, but here we will stay.
That one simple sentence had just sealed their fate, nothing to do, but wait and wait,
wait for the enemy thirsting with hate.

Olly

Olly is my dog, much more he is my joy,
he's a trusted friend, a brother in kind,
my four-legged lovely boy.
For over seven years he's calmed my fears,
his antics make me smile.
From a mischievous pup to a senior dog,
unique in his character and style.

Twice a day in wind, snow, ice and rain,
we walk the fields, the lakeside paths,
the muddy, rough terrain.
He is a hunter by trade, a killing machine,
though not bereft of grace.
He gives them a start, the squirrel, duck
and fox, but sometimes wins the race.

Olly is my dog, much more he is my joy.

New Age?

And so the new age dawned or so they promised,
though when the dust had settled it looked very much the same.
And beyond the empty platitudes of reason
starkly exposed the guilt of those to blame.

As for the emergence of expected prosperity and riches,
the common man has made false sacrifice in vain.
To all intents the future harmony cruelly shattered
and existence threatened by the continued heaviness of pain.

The men who conjured up their own images
gloat in exultation when the curtain call is prolonged.
The innocent actors their ovation quite surrendered,
stand stage-struck by the enormity of their wrongs.

Great empires through slavery were created,
confusion is the father of the never-ending scene.
Though the cameo role for the devil is intended,
the audience don't know what might have been.

The outward strength a testimony to propaganda,
more utterly false prophets to greedily devour the land.
One all-powerful Master far more savage than the last one,
the ultimate system of man's inhumanity to man.

First Doubts

It is suddenly the airport, arriving home from Spain after that first
    holiday we enjoyed,
when told of the death of your cat, you were more relieved than sad.
Strange how that feeling of your lack of feeling remained in my mind,
though, of course, I buried it deep, just like you buried the cat.

Was it then, so long before the fall, when I was still your only
salvation, that I knew my days were numbered?
How could one mangy cat which I had hardly seen, hardly knew,
awake such a sense of loss in a love so young?
Still it did, and I remembered.

Lady

Lady, auburn hair, cascading onto sun-hued skin,
her appealing eyes detached yet so aware,
although only the studied flicker of her brow
gives hint of what or who or where.

Sensitive, unconcerned, oblivious to humdrum cloud she sits,
the relaxed appearance a camouflage of see-through design.
No shelter yet built can deflect that gaze of hers,
gently condescending, provocative, intent, yet strangely benign.

Gone

What is left now she has gone? People say life must go on,
but they never knew that special feeling that grasped my entire being.
In the void she left there's only a distant haze of life before,
and now I feel the aching loss and, what's more, the heart-tearing pain.
What would I give to hear her joyous laughter again?

Did I know, could I see, what life with her would ultimately offer?
It matters not as I am destined to live in a bad dream without her.
My mind will never shut out the joy, the look of love, beauty, coy.
I know I could carry on, forget the past, change my outlook,
but I miss that special, timeless something that angel of my soul
    took.

Dawn Rendezvous

I see you in the long freezing dawn, wandering across the frost-etched grass, confident in your manner.
You look towards me (or is it beyond me?) your frozen breath shimmering over me.
I, meanwhile, am reliving that same dream but desperately seeking a different ending.

Please don't go, I plead, as your silent acquiescence and your fading footmarks even then prove an illusion.
Like a frightened deer in the white glare of sudden headlights, I see your eyes wide open, I feel your love, I cry for us.
It is all at once so cold, so still, the scene so completely and utterly empty.

I prepare for the reprise tomorrow.

All Done

There was a time in earlier rhyme when I was young and sure,
that hooked me up and turned me on and let my high hopes soar.
But now I'm old, much less bold and life's meaning seems unclear,
I remember with joy those earlier days when the furthest thought
	was fear.
And so I write, but now no bite, the enthusiasm has waned,
and life goes on and on and on, till only death has gained.

A Public House in England

Cluttered glasses upon beer-stained tables,
old men peruse surroundings and stumble,
rivulets forming on oaken floors awash with
the flotsam of night's entertainment past.

Cracked glass windows gaze in disbelief as narrow-
minded purveyors of profit reap their soul-destroying rewards.
Vessels empty or half-empty of liver fatal disease stand
in disarray, testimony to yet one more night of false hopes.

Outside, ashtrays fall unheeded in the consuming moments
of the evening's close.
One more cigarette, its cancer ally cheated, burns to an
inglorious end.
Everything is quiet, all sounds of merriment gone, the echoes
of distant laughter signal yet another wasted night.

London Life

Waterloo Bridge at half past eight,
The early summer sun unheeded by commuters hurrying, scurrying,
    often late;
a railway guard in an unguarded moment stubs out his first of the day,
shakes his head and in a beaten, dismissive manner, shuffles slowly away
as a suspicious pigeon with wary eyes and frightened claws scans the
    tarmac
for sight of scraps to eat,
seemingly not aware of the river Thames and the history so close to his
constantly moving, scurrying feet.

The Thames where Drake plied his trade, where Raleigh set off to
    literally lose his head,
the river where every Englishman is so proud to recall the moments
    when the good king Charles in his pomp took boat instead,
to fight that fire, those papist flames, to stop the inferno, to stem the
    flames,
to make a stand against the city he loved, nearly dying, never dead.

So, mass commuters, as you approach your long, fraught journey home,
remember on whose sacred ground you tread,
for the bones of many a proud English tar are deep beneath
the silted soil, the concrete pavements, the high rise apartments,
the stench of the dead.

Caribbean Queen

Beneath sun-filled skies of the deepest hue,
I feel the warmth, the joy of you,
beside the palm trees so heavy in spread,
I trace the sand where you had tread.

You are my exciting sunshine fantasy.
You are my wildest exotic dream.
You are all my lifetime longings.
You are my one and only Caribbean Queen.

Visions Of Old Age

The old man's eyes strain heavy year-laden brows,
a water mist of lost opportunities flood the overwhelming thoughts of death,
for an age the embittered glare strikes a hollow chord in the empty room,
senses failing, body yearning, but youth is imprisoned by the inglorious past.

No new worlds conquered, the sun and moon still our only everlasting light,
pauses, laughs, long, clear and angry in sudden awareness of approaching doom,
slaps emaciated thigh, rises to greet the new passing of the night,
a deeply lined, suffocating last look on three score years of woe.

Empty sunlight, strong and unmerciful, strikes the dead body,
passes over and glows beyond.

You

I didn't know what love was until I met you.
I didn't know what happiness meant, but now I do.
I only knew that you opened my eyes.
You made me believe, made me realise.

You overwhelmed my senses, you opened my mind.
Filled me with such fervour I thought I'd never find.
You breached my defences, you made me feel so whole.
You are my mentor, my lover, my angel, my soul.

Highams Lake

As the swans return to Highams in their pomp and majesty once more,
and the windswept trees salute them from the comfort of the shore,
when the ground underfoot is softening and the snow is on the wane,
and the pale spring sun shining weakly heralds winter's last refrain.

As the gossamer-thin ice is cracking and the wildlife wakes anew,
and the lake gleams in golden splendour, its cold dark days nearly
     through,
when the cygnets have received their orders and to the skies they soar,
and their parents in all their beauty command the tranquil waters
     once more.

The Ghosts

Were we ever of this world, have you ever felt
that fast flowing rhythm of the afterlife, the dark?
Or are we simply more fresh kindling. glowing
as the coffins slowly melt?

We were the wind, whilst it was blowing,
through the skirting, in the cupboard and on the plains,
summoning the prophets, calling the wise men,
fanning the flames.

We were the snow whilst the blizzard rages,
whilst the watchman gazes as the world turns raw,
covering the new graves,
we creep off the stage through that creaking door.

We were the sun whilst the sun was shining,
illuminating our near forgotten past,
burning our never to happen future,
yellowing the parchment in which we were cast.

We were the fire, whilst the fire was burning,
warming the now scattered bones,
charring the blood black with ash,
cremating what flesh remains, smothering our useless moans.

We were the clouds, whilst the sky was cloudy,
lost worlds in their centre of despair.
See the sleek, round, brown plague rats,
the ships beached and helpless that carried them there.

We were life and now we are not, we are no more.
We were that which came before and died before.
We were all we were and never ever more.

Checkmate

Do you remember those games of chess?
I will never forget them, never forget you.
I recall so much laughter, so much concentration,
so much wine,
through a haze of cigarette smoke, we played the game
of love,
caressing each piece with our fingers, with our eyes and with
our minds.

I always started the stronger with a superior strategy known only to
    me,
yet you grew more confident game by game,
second-guessing my plans, seizing on my inherent weakness, your
white queen devouring my leaden defence.
You so loved your victories, those late night triumphs, your
eyes blazing with pleasure.
Nobody else remembers those nights, but I remember them and I
remember you.

My Neighbour's Cat

That damned cat, sat where he sat and that was that,
car bonnet, roof, boot or wing,
sat where he sat,
did his own thing.

All the dogs cowered, so very afraid of the fright.
Our road he owned and no-one dared fight
that big ball of fur with the God-given right
to sit there so powerful, dawn, day or night.

He stared at us with disdain when out near our feet
knew that we knew he ruled all the street.
Never missed an opportunity to prove so elite,
always the master, his kingdom complete.

That damned cat, so full of life, so certain, so assured,
wish he was still with us, still feared yet adored.

Foolish

A man once said of my rhymes
that they offered no hope, no joy,
no laughter,
but only despair, decay and disaster.
I raised my melancholy eyes and managed
a wry smile,
saying, my friend, you have missed the
whole design.
It's not my saddest thoughts you can see,
but thine.

Heaven to Me

You are heaven to me, every part perfection,
a bright, dazzling light illuminating my life,
an angel of such beauty, of such joy and laughter
the antidote to this cruel, cold, desperate world.

With you, no doubts, no uncertainty, no fear or despair.
Instead hope and conviction, happiness and passion.
You are heaven to me, every day delightful,
every moment exhilarating, every second a first.

You are heaven to me, every day so sure, so certain,
a chorus of love from deep within,
like an open flower of stunning vibrant colour.
You are sanctuary to me, my isle of tranquillity,
my haven of serenity, my heaven on earth.

Images

Moonlit river straddled by trembling oaks,
dappled rays peering through cloudless shadows
of forgotten growth,
glades surrounded by tall brown cloaks,
highlighted water a deep blue mauve.

Sifted through gnarled, mossed boughs heavy with a
foliage of decay,
unseeing eyes of invisible owls camouflaged in
Nature's sober way,
watch fox, ferret and stoat, grey shadows in the night,
mingle as in mutual confusion beneath the moon,
while God flooding the scene with unreflected light.

A foretaste of the day breaking soon, when earthly freedom
will once more hide its face
beneath the exterior of wooded dreams and leaf-covered velvet
grass like lace,
making a golden carpet rivalling the stream.
All movement stopped, a silent, deathly stillness reigns,
peace and quiet at last as the early morning sunrays soothe,
focus on the motionless forest as even the river ceases to move.

Missing You

So people ask me do I miss you?
Do I miss you? Does the dawn break, does the sun set,
does the moon shine, the rain fall, the earth spin?

Oh yes I miss you, I miss you so much.
I miss every single, lonely, aching hour spent without you.

It's been like a cold winter's morning without the crisp white frost.
It's like a spring day with no promise of the glorious summer to come.

And though it wasn't always perfect, and we had moments of regret,
I would willingly trade ten years of my life without you for one
    minute back in your arms.

Yes I miss you, I miss you so much.

A Daughter's Plea

From my very first breath, you were there and have been the only constant ever since.
You nursed me through all my childhood fears, guided, nurtured and protected me for all those early years.
Now, with great sorrow, I find those roles reversed and it is I that must care and cry for you.
These tears I hide, I fear completely in vain, you are so well aware despite your pain.

Of course, I won't ever give up on you, just as you never did with me.
My love for you, my memories of us will remain when all the photos have turned to dust.
I so hope that we will be together once more but in some other place and some other time.
I always will be yours and you will always be the mother of mine.

Noble King

So rest in peace at last our noble warrior king.
Your long years of solitude now are gone
and your name shall be exalted throughout the land
as the slanderous barbs of history are finally proven wrong.

Of pure Plantagenet stock, of royal lineage proud,
you were a beacon of noble spirit, brave,
and against the uneducated words your reputation stole,
you will rise in glory from that meanest grave.

So rest in peace you proud son of York.
Your courage and wisdom did never fail
through the centuries of such harshest falsehoods
to finally show the truth of the third Richard's tale.

One Day Soon

Do not pity me for you will soon be old too.
Do not think that because I stoop and shuffle and sigh
that I was not once as lithe and supple as you.
I may well be lined, wrinkled, grey,
but not so long ago I was young, alert and keen.
Picture yourself in the rapid passing of years to come.
You too will feel what to you I seem.

Bird on the Wing

Bird on the wing, can you really fly and leave your heartaches
　　behind you?
Carry mine, seize their content, confound their content,
exorcise this devil within me,
fly it to the highest mountain range, release it over forgotten valleys
of an unseen age,
litter the remains of a memorial pyre of senseless devotion to life,
bear the weight with fortitude beneath your feathers, fear not black
Satan's evil driving wind.
Remember the eye that awaits your return.

Disperse my tears in glistening lakes of sheer despair,
climb above the clouds and ever higher with my dreams,
speed high, don't fail my inspiration.
Singe those wings on the sun's ever burning luminous rays,
melt my desires, charcoal my bridges, release my senses
and fly, fly as far as you dare.

Bird on the wing, can you really leave your heartaches behind you?
Don't look back, they are still waiting there for me.

Angel

Wild eyed beauty, face divine,
lovely lady, will you be mine?
Lithe, elegant figure, enchanting smile,
captivating angel, how you beguile.

With one look you melt my heart,
increase my pulse rate, tear me apart.
A word of encouragement is all I desire,
to burn my ego upon your fire.

End Game

It's nearly dawn or so the birds believe,
and if it is, I've sat the entire night
with little thought and no result
to shield me from the morning light,
which, though unasked, will soon appear
and wipe away the empty time,
the cold regret, the puzzled years,
as though we never actually met
in that different world before the tears.

Reflections of War

A fallen soldier, who am I to receive oration when I die?
If a memory is left of me, tend it well for, you see,
no roses grow to mark my grave,
no, nothing but earth, save for a rusty tin helmet,
not even mine,
no cross or name, without a sign.

Perhaps in years to come you'll find
where many perished of my kind,
and for their country time do spend
under rich brown mud where only sign of blood
tells of how they gave their all, to never hear in the hall
when their bemedalled officer will tell
how he beat the enemy from here to hell,
and make this whole vile war seem as though it's a game
where all honourable men taste glory and fame.

I know different.

My Love

As even subtle airs and knowing looks
seem not to deter such wanton thoughts,
can you ever, pray, consider me
your beau, your lover, your ever sought?

My earnest ways I do decry,
through lack of guile and many doubts
do but endear you in my dreams ,
into love I stumble, of love I shout.

Is your countenance of such disdain,
a cloud, a malevolence of sorry sight?
Or may I dare the notion now, declare
that my yearning is such found delight?

Wild Country

When late summer's sun has slipped away,
when the first sign of autumn beckons,
on such a night I sense the feel
of those lonely, windswept Brecons.

Where nature sits and time stands still,
where the wilderness is the glory,
there I long to take my ease
with the cloudless sky above me.

A Dog's Life

Oh, how to live the life of a dog.
Oh, how to be so free.
No parking fines, no income tax,
and no bloody V.A.T.

Oh, how to run so effortlessly, so proud,
so fleet, so sure.
Oh, the sounds, the smells, the thrill of
the chase, the freedom I'd adore.

Oh, how to be without cars, the shopping,
the clock-watching, the phone.
Just a bowl of water, a handful of biscuits,
and if I'm lucky, a bone.

Oh why, my Master thinks I'm trained,
when I hear his shouts and just ignore!
Yet I'll still wag my tail and get a reward.
For he loves me, of that I'm sure.

Air Hostess

So, you're going to be an air hostess, top level waitress,
to the mass of secretive Arabs and their kids and their mess.
In three inch heels at over thirty thousand feet,
checking over oxygen, strapping Grand Viziers in their seats.

Oriental cities, aflame and afar.
High-flying aircraft, in touch with the stars.
Bourbon and brandy, Bangkok and Hong Kong.
Pre-heated lunches, business suit, or sarong.

So, you want to see America, then you will have to be high.
Either drugged up or mugged up, better off in the sky.
It's plain to see you're very keen on the captain, he's such a dear.
His eyesight's gone, he drinks a lot, you'll find out he's queer.

So, you want to be glamorous, Canada next, then the Med.
If you're lucky, you'll avoid shellshock taking an Iraqi to bed.
Remember Mecca is not only bingo, this jackpot's not such fun.
Keep your prayer mat by your bedside, right next to your gun.

Oil-enriched oligarchs, the new favoured elite.
Pampered as princes, aloof in their seats.
First class, but last chance a sheikh to impress.
Dreamland with olives, the acrid smell of success.

Dark Times

Winter trees, bare, stark, revealing.
Threatening skies like a cold heart unfeeling.
Last of the summer wine, end of a chapter.
Life once renewed again, so elusive to recapture.

Dark times the future brings, memories fade to dust.
Different journeys to intrigue upon, no one left to trust.
And when the warmth of the sun returns, will our paths meet again?
Or like the ice prove transparent and crack beneath the strain?

Death by Taxi

Black taxi, a ghostly dark vehicle driven at breakneck speed
through rain-laden streets where not a soul is perceived.
Carrying rat-faced rejects in comfort and style,
wheels effortlessly gliding, meter ticking every mile.

It's a one way ticket to nowhere fast.
All obstacles avoided to prevent being last.
To the haven where all the best vehicles strive,
at the end of the journey, life's last long drive.

Empty

What is left now she has gone?
People smile, life must go on.
But they never knew the special feeling
that grasped my whole being.

In the void she's left, there is only a drunken haze
of life before.
And now I feel the loss and the heart-tearing pain.
What would I give for her fresh laughter again?

Did I know, could I see, what life could offer?
Now, I never will without her.
My mind will never shut out her joy,
her Byzantine face, aggressive, coy.
I could carry on, I could change my outlook,
but I will never have that special feeling
that angel of my soul took.

Faking It

The leaves are tumbling from the trees,
as the memories are flowing through my mind.
The rain is falling on my hair.
You have stolen the happy times.

My darling, do not look so sad,
for the sorrow I feel is enough for two.
I can't forget the times we shared,
or the great love I still feel for you.

As soon as the snow has melted away,
my weary heart will cease to ache.
And as the birds return to sing,
then my laughter, I will fake.

All too quickly our time has passed,
the fun and laughter, the sorrow too.
And I must face the bitter truth at last,
of a future without the joy of you.

Forward

Take the trench, kill the man.
Cut his throat, wipe your hand.
Leave his body, take his gun.
On again, quickly run.

Climb the wall, jump the ditch.
Enemy fires, shoot the bitch.
Don't wait now, on you go.
Who have you shot, friend or foe?

Don't answer back, got no time.
Him or you, and no crime.
War's a game and you're a pawn.
Wounds stitched up, nearly dawn.

Back to the start, grab a bite.
Clean your knife, start to write.
Count the cost, see no gain.
Open fire, on again.

Night Raid

Grey, gloom, spreading mist.
Groping figures linger, as if it's dawn
when death's cold comfort beckons.
Whilst through the mud, cold and forlorn,
shivering men lurch and heave like drunken wrecks
on a roaring, rampant sea.
Where tossed back and forth among red waves
fall as dead men to be.

Our Love

It was only a period of time, a brief interlude,
a mere hiccough in history, not of enough importance
to cause a murmur on the most sensitive of Richter scales.
But it was you and me, it was our lives, our thoughts, our
dreams, our love.

You were then, as you are now, the greatest influence in my
life, of my life.
Loving you was not a temporary arrangement. If the time and
circumstances were right then, they are right now.
Without you, I don't exist, I can't exist, I won't exist.

The Body in Question

Your eyes entranced me, those expressive, frightened glimpses into your soul.
Your lips excited me, and I defy anyone who has kissed them, as I did, to contradict me.
Your mouth I adored, for surely the ambrosia of the Gods never tasted so sweet and fulfilling.

Your breasts I worshipped, caressing those soft round orbs crowned with the proud ruby fruits that epitomised your femininity, your sexuality.
Hundreds of times I gazed into your eyes, kissed you fully on the mouth, teased your lips with mine, and aroused your breasts before we made love.

You were the epitome of a goddess, the sensual siren of my dreams.

Thinking of You

Sitting here lonely, thinking of you.
Wondering if you're with someone new,
who tells you stories, makes you smile,
increases your heartbeat, admires your style.

I hope you miss me, although I doubt very much
whether you think of my kisses or my touch.
I long to see you, but then I don't,
too frightened you'll believe, and then that you won't.

It's no good pretending, I've lost you for good.
We might have been happy. I am sure that we would.
So now it's all over, but my love remains true.
Sitting here lonely, thinking of you.

Waiting

Though you're chasing impossible dreams beneath the sun
in distant lands,
I will sit and wait for you, like Man has sat since time began.
And when your hopes have passed you by, cruelly shattered,
interest spent,
then I trust you will see the truth of life within this sad lament.

If we, together, could face the world through all the pain of
loneliness,
then surely life would start to matter, despite the long felt bitterness?
For all the days I thought your thoughts, suffered the agonies of pain
anew,
I would give ten thousand more for just one hour spent with you.

Where's the Girl?

Where's the girl?
The house is empty without her laughter,
uneasy, desolate, since her swift departure.

Where's the girl?
Who used to smile that contagious, winning smile,
flutter those eyelashes, bewitch, and beguile?

Where's the girl?
Her long, dark hair a luxuriant tumble, gloss of fire.
Her eye-catching figure, curvaceous, full of an inner
burning desire.

Who Are You?

Who are you, lying there, motionless in your crisp, white, spotless shroud,
your unseeing eyes, your waxen features, so oblivious to the ticking clock,
you who were once so regimented, so time conscious, now not hearing that
monotonous, mocking tick-tock?

Who are you, what distant vivid memories were you part of,
what emotions, how many scenes of laughter and tears did you see
when now the whispered, mournful dirges of the wind fail to herald
a time still to be?

We know who you are and soon who we will be too.
You are our childhood, you are our prime, you are our dark old age,
you are our mothers' milk, our nursery rhymes, our petty crimes, our
Fathers' drunken rage.

You are the architect, the baker, the farmer and the guide,
the craftsman, the hunter, the gardener, the judge.
You are the office boy, that fresh-faced youth and his teenage pregnant bride.

You are our beauty, our elegance, our self-respect, our pride,
our childrens' schemes, our most impassioned dreams,
the hope, the glory, the turning of the tide.

You are also our nightmares, the type that shake us awake.
You are the senseless void, the tragic waste, the dementia haze,
the one pill we can't take.

You are our backache, our shaking limbs, our cancer, our strain,
our heart defects, our hardened arteries, our dementia, our stress.
You are our most secret fears, our silent tears, our most decisive pain.

Life

What is life? Is it merely a pebble on the beach or just one grain of sand?
A fleeting burst of sunlight, a sudden shower over before the sun returns?
A passing thought like a ship on a perilous sea?
A definitive voyage on a short journey to the land?

Is it the waking of the dawn chorus stifled in mid song?
The brief interlude of happiness between our birth and death?
The finality of the rainbow at the end of a storm?
The inevitably of the passing days, the carnival moving on?

Is it so outrageously pointless, such little time to endear,
that sometimes we wish we could slow the process down,
to freeze a frame, to pause a while, to stop the life cycle turning,
to step outside from our mortality, to live without the fear?

We Shall Meet Again

We shall meet again, though the years have passed and the trusted
   landscape totally transformed.
We will see our faces, hear our stories, feel the calm, the familiarity
   of our smiles,
the affection that passage of time can never ever mask.

We shall meet again and more, it will be as it was, it will always be
   summer and it will always be fine.
We of such good heart, of youthfulness renewed, of a future
   unquestioned, of happiness now so sure.

We shall meet gain and we will sit at the very top table, on God's
   right hand.
We will count our blessings and count our friends, enjoy the endless
   days and never frown or have cause for anger,
but take our fill in this exciting new bounteous land.

We shall meet again for so it is written, and in our prime,
we will see each other and have such fun, from the dawning of the
   day
to the muttering of the night,
We, my friend, will be sipping ambrosia and taking our leisure for
   the remainder of time.

NOTES

Behind

'Curses and Verses'

Although the majority of poems featured in this book are love poems, there are some I wrote due to particular circumstances and situations that have occurred in my life and touched my emotions.

These range from the sadness of a friend's dying mother, the love of my dog, to the beauty of a wildlife scene.

What follows is a brief synopsis on the thinking and reasons behind the writing of these poems.

Behind

'A Daughter's Prayer'

The mother of a very dear friend had become extremely ill with cancer, and one day, with her mother's condition rapidly deteriorating, my friend and I took our dogs on a very emotional walk, and she told me of her fears for the future.

This chat inspired me to write the poem.

Tragically, her mother died only a few days later, and to this day, my friend has never seen this poem.

Behind

'Air Hostess'

When I was a young man, my ex-wife had two very attractive younger sisters, who both had brief periods working as air hostesses on the Royal Jordanian airline.

I wrote this poem in part to warn of the potential downfalls, although my fears subsequently, and happily, proved unfounded!

Behind

'My Neighbour's Cat'

This cat really did exist.

It did terrify the neighbourhood wildlife and caused my dog, Olly, more frustration than any other creature alive, as it resolutely refused to show any fear of him.

Tragically killed too early by a car as it went to greet its owner, but never forgotten.

Behind

'Olly' and 'It's a Dog's Life'

Olly is our seven-year old German Shorthaired Pointer, a large, noble-looking dog, who is treated entirely as one of the family, and boy, doesn't he know it and takes advantage of it!

However, he is a great companion on our twice-daily walks and definitely helps to keep me fit, healthy, and constantly on my toes!

Not always a dog for the faint-hearted, but also a great favourite with the ladies who find him handsome. And they do say that dogs resemble their masters – not true!

Behind

'Highams Lake'

Highams Park (formerly known as Highams) is an area of north east London that borders on the county of Essex. It is, therefore, conveniently located to gain speedy access to the centre of the capital, whilst being a stone's throw away from the tranquillity of Epping Forest.

Highams Park lake, park, and surrounding forest is an area I know very well, having walked my dog, Olly, here almost twice daily for the last seven years.

One day in early spring, when the mist was swirling and the snow melting, I was inspired to go home and put pen to paper.

The swans have always been a feature of the lake as long as I can remember and the pair currently in residence has literally fought off many would-be successors over the years.

Behind

'We Shall Meet Again'

Another dog-walking friend of mine recounted the story of her dog, Sheba.

She had owned Sheba for quite some years and said that they enjoyed a very special bond. She told me that Sheba always seemed to know when she felt low, ill, or lonely and would comfort and make her feel much better.

The day eventually came, after some sixteen years of very close companionship, when Sheba died. My friend was distraught and so overwhelmed with grief that, for a time, life did not seem to be worth living.

Then one night, Sheba appeared to her in a dream and said, "Don't worry about me, I am fine". Although a non-believer in spiritual/religious matters, my friend was comforted, and the experience undoubtedly helped her to eventually ease her grief.

Some weeks later, she accompanied a spiritualist friend to a show given by a medium. During the show, the medium suddenly looked straight at her and said, "I can see a white dog called Sheepa, Shaba, no, Sheba, and she says that she has already let you know not to worry. She is fine, but repeats that again. 'Please don't grieve anymore, I am happy and well'."

That story, told by a non-believer, really affected me and I went home and began to wonder if I lost my dog or a person really close to me, just how I would feel.

This incident became the inspiration for my poem, 'We Shall Meet Again', and I really hope that this will be the case when we all finally meet our maker.

Behind

'Noble King'

From a very young age I have been fascinated by history, in particular, the medieval period and the turbulent times later named the Wars of the Roses.

Richard III is my favourite monarch, despite being much maligned, from Shakespeare and Thomas More onwards, as the wicked, crouchback uncle who had his two innocent nephews murdered in the Tower of London.

The evidence for this crime is, in my opinion, far from conclusive, and I am firmly of the belief that had he been victorious at the Battle of Bosworth, he would have proven himself to be one of the best kings to ever sit on the throne of England.

More recently, I have been transfixed by the finding of his skeleton buried beneath a car park in Leicester, and hope that he may now be given a proper burial, respecting his rank. I hope that this will take place in his beloved York Minster.

Behind

'A Public House in England'

This poem was written on my 21st birthday after a somewhat boozy night in a local pub.

Although I subsequently enjoyed a huge, joint twenty-first birthday party with my cousin, this night obviously lingered on in my mind and prompted my rather hazy recollections.

Of course, a lot has happened to pubs in the intervening years, most of it for the better, and there are very few of the "spit and sawdust" type now remaining.

Behind

'The Battlefield', 'Forward', 'Reflections of War' and 'Night Raid'

This quartet of my earliest poems was inspired by the television documentary series, *'The Great War'*, which was broadcast in the mid-sixties.

The thought of so many men being senselessly killed for just a few yards of territory really affected me as a young boy.

My feelings were much later brilliantly brought to the public's interest in the BBC comedy series, *'Blackadder'*.

A request from the author

I'd like to ask a favour.

If you have enjoyed this book (and I certainly hope you have), then I would love it if you not only tell your friends and family about it, but also leave a great review on those websites where it is available for sale.

You can also send me your review and get in touch with me via my website. Simply visit http://www.andrewcaseypoet.com and fill out the Contact form. I would be extremely grateful.

Many thanks,
    Andrew Casey